This book is belongs to

_____

Hi, I am a therapist at CAPA. We are so glad you are here! Please make yourself at home.

What's your name?

Nice to meet you!
An adult who cares
about you thought it
would be a good idea
for you to come to
CAPA. I am so glad they
did.

When most kids come to CAPA, they spend time playing.

While you are playing, you can talk about anything you want. Our therapists are really good listeners.

Our job when you are with us is to spend time with you and just focus on you.

Let me show you some of the places you can play while you are here.

This is the playroom. It is filled with so many fun things to do!

It has all kinds of toys! You can be anything you want here!

This is our playground. This is a fun place to be active. Sometimes we talk about our feelings while we play, too.

Sometimes feelings are so powerful it helps to talk about them.

You have the power to
use your feelings to
become stronger.

No feeling is too big.
No feeling is too small.
Sometimes we all need
someone to talk to
about how we feel
inside.

CAPA is a safe place.
When you are here,
you matter the most.

When our time is up, I will help you get to the lobby safely. We will say goodbye until I see you next time.

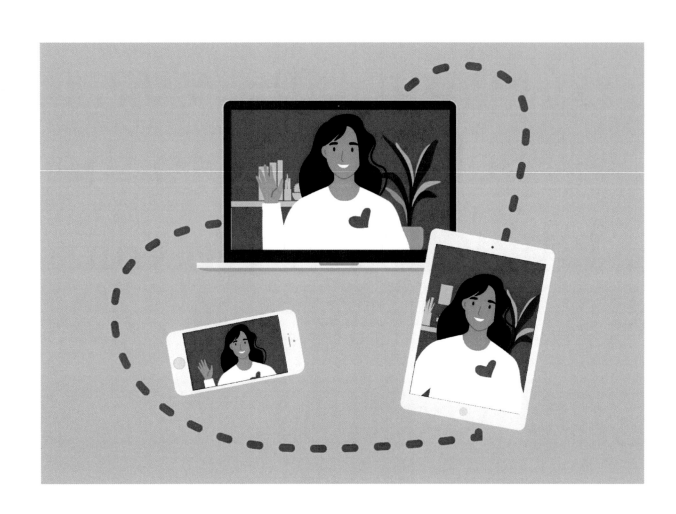

Just in case you can't come to the office and we need to meet on phone, iPad, or computer, it's okay.

We may be not get to see each other face to face, but we can still talk and play!

We look forward to
seeing you again soon!

Contact Us

CAPA Independence
503 East 23rd Street
Independence, MO 64055
816-252-8388

CAPA Kansas City
4240 Blue Ridge Boulevard, Suite 515
Kansas City, MO 64133
816-601-0550

www.capacares.org

Resources

Child Abuse and Neglect Hotline
1-800-392-3738 (in Missouri)
573-751-3448 (outside of Missouri)

National Mental Health Hotline
Free & Confidential 27/7 Assistance
1-866-903-3787

United Way of Greater Kansas City
Free access to thousands of resources 24/7
Call 2-1-1

Made in the USA
Middletown, DE
22 July 2022

69755302R00022